Mediterranean Seafood Cookbook

Delicious Mediterranean Flavors and Recipes to Savor the Bounty of the Sea

While every precaution has been taken in the preparation of this book, the publisher assumes no responsibility for errors or omissions, or for damages resulting from the use of the information contained herein.

MEDITERRANEAN SEAFOOD COOKBOOK

First edition. November 17, 2023.

ISBN: 979-8223470236

Written by Sammy Andrews.

Table of Contents

Sammy Andrews

Chapter 1: Introduction to Mediterranean Cuisine

The Mediterranean Sea, with its azure waters and diverse coastlines, has been the cradle of civilization and a melting pot of cultures for centuries. But it's not just the stunning scenery that makes this region special; it's the food. The Mediterranean diet is renowned for its health benefits and exquisite flavors, and at its heart lies an abundance of seafood.

In this chapter, we'll delve into the essence of Mediterranean cuisine, exploring its history, philosophy, and the key elements that make it so irresistible. Whether you're a seasoned cook or a newcomer to this culinary tradition, understanding the fundamentals of Mediterranean cuisine will set the stage for a seafood adventure like no other.

The Mediterranean Diet: A Healthy Tradition

The Mediterranean diet isn't merely a way of eating; it's a way of life. It's a nutritional pattern rooted in the dietary habits of the countries bordering the Mediterranean Sea, such as Greece, Italy, Spain, and Southern France. What sets this diet apart is its emphasis on fresh, whole foods that are not only delicious but also incredibly good for your health.

Key Features of the Mediterranean Diet

Abundance of Fresh Vegetables: The Mediterranean diet places a heavy emphasis on vegetables like tomatoes, cucumbers, bell peppers, and leafy greens. These vegetables are not just side dishes; they often take center stage in Mediterranean recipes.

Healthy Fats: Olive oil is the primary source of fat in Mediterranean cuisine. It's rich in monounsaturated fats, which have been linked to heart health and longevity. Nuts and seeds also provide healthy fats.

Lean Proteins: While seafood is a star player, lean meats like poultry and occasional servings of red meat are included in moderation.

Whole Grains: Whole grains like bulgur, couscous, and whole wheat bread are staples, providing a steady source of energy and fiber.

Fresh Fruits: Fresh fruits such as figs, grapes, and citrus are enjoyed as snacks and desserts.

Moderate Dairy: Yogurt and cheese, particularly feta and goat cheese, are enjoyed but in moderation.

Wine in Moderation: A glass of red wine with meals, particularly in Mediterranean countries, is not just a beverage but a cultural tradition.

Herbs and Spices: Herbs and spices like basil, oregano, rosemary, and garlic are used liberally, adding depth and flavor to dishes without the need for excessive salt.

The Role of Seafood in Mediterranean Cooking

Mediterranean cuisine is inseparable from the sea. With its vast coastline and proximity to the Mediterranean Sea, it's no wonder that seafood plays a central role in this culinary tradition. The Mediterranean Sea teems with an array of fish and shellfish, providing an endless source of inspiration for Mediterranean cooks.

Why Choose Seafood?

Health Benefits: Seafood is rich in omega-3 fatty acids, which have been linked to reduced risk of heart disease and improved cognitive function.

Versatility: From delicate white fish to robust shellfish, seafood offers a wide range of textures and flavors to work with.

Sustainability: Many Mediterranean countries are champions of sustainable fishing practices, ensuring that seafood remains available for generations to come.

Cultural Significance: For coastal communities, seafood isn't just food; it's a way of life, steeped in tradition and culinary expertise.

Flavor: Seafood adds a distinctive and delightful taste to Mediterranean dishes, whether it's the brininess of mussels in a tomato sauce or the delicate sweetness of grilled squid.

Regional Influences in Mediterranean Cuisine

The Mediterranean is a vast region with diverse cultures and culinary traditions. While there are common threads that tie Mediterranean cuisine together, each country and even specific regions within those countries have their own unique dishes and flavors.

Some Regional Highlights:

Greek Cuisine: Known for dishes like moussaka, souvlaki, and baklava, Greek cuisine combines fresh seafood with olives, feta cheese, and aromatic herbs.

Italian Cuisine: Italian coastal regions are famous for their seafood pasta dishes, such as spaghetti alle vongole (clam pasta) and seafood risotto. The use of tomatoes, garlic, and olive oil is prevalent.

Spanish Cuisine: Spain offers an array of seafood paellas, vibrant gazpacho, and tapas like grilled octopus and gambas al ajillo (garlic shrimp). Spanish cuisine varies greatly from region to region, reflecting the country's diverse landscapes.

Southern France: The cuisine of Southern France, particularly Provence, showcases the flavors of the Mediterranean herbs like thyme and rosemary, often paired with seafood such as bouillabaisse and seafood aioli.

As you embark on your Mediterranean seafood journey, keep in mind that the beauty of this cuisine lies in its diversity. You can draw inspiration from all these regions to create a rich tapestry of flavors on your own plate.

In the upcoming chapters, we'll explore essential ingredients, cooking techniques, and a wide array of recipes that capture the essence of Mediterranean seafood cuisine. Whether you're preparing a quick weeknight meal or hosting a special gathering, these recipes will transport your taste buds to the shores of the Mediterranean.

Now that we've set the stage, let's dive into the essential ingredients for Mediterranean seafood cooking in Chapter 2.

Chapter 2: Essential Ingredients for Mediterranean Seafood

Mediterranean cuisine is all about celebrating the natural flavors of fresh, wholesome ingredients. In this chapter, we'll explore the fundamental elements that form the backbone of Mediterranean seafood cooking. From the importance of choosing the right seafood to the liquid gold of the Mediterranean kitchen – olive oil – and the aromatic herbs and spices that elevate dishes to new heights, you'll gain a deeper understanding of the key components that make Mediterranean seafood cuisine so extraordinary.

Fresh vs. Frozen Seafood: Making the Right Choice

Choosing the right seafood is crucial for any Mediterranean dish. While frozen seafood can be convenient and of high quality, fresh seafood often takes center stage in Mediterranean cooking. Here, we'll help you navigate the choices and make informed decisions.

The Benefits of Fresh Seafood

Flavor: Fresh seafood boasts a vibrant, clean taste that can't be replicated by frozen alternatives.

Texture: Fresh seafood typically has a firmer, more pleasing texture compared to frozen options.

Versatility: Fresh seafood can be used in a wider range of recipes, from grilling to ceviche.

Local and Seasonal: Opting for fresh seafood from local markets ensures you're supporting sustainable practices and enjoying ingredients at their peak.

When to Choose Frozen Seafood

Convenience: Frozen seafood is often more accessible and convenient, making it a valuable pantry staple.

Extended Shelf Life: Frozen seafood can be stored for longer periods, reducing waste.

Availability: Some species are only available frozen, making it the only option for certain dishes.

Tips for Buying Fresh Seafood

Visit Local Fish Markets: Seek out local fish markets for the freshest catches, as they often source directly from fishermen.

Look for Signs of Freshness: Bright, clear eyes; firm flesh; and a clean, ocean-like smell are indicators of fresh seafood.

Ask Questions: Don't hesitate to ask your fishmonger about the origin and sustainability of the seafood they offer.

Consider Sustainability: Choose seafood that is sustainably sourced to support healthy oceans and marine ecosystems.

Olive Oil: The Heart of Mediterranean Cooking

Olive oil is more than just a cooking oil in Mediterranean cuisine; it's a cornerstone of flavor and nutrition. Known as "liquid gold," olive oil is a key ingredient in many Mediterranean seafood dishes, and its use dates back thousands of years.

Types of Olive Oil

Extra Virgin Olive Oil: This premium grade has a robust flavor and is best used for dressings, drizzling, and finishing dishes.

Virgin Olive Oil: Slightly lower in quality than extra virgin, it's still excellent for cooking and sautéing.

Regular Olive Oil: A blend of virgin and refined oils, this is a good all-purpose cooking oil.

Why Olive Oil?

Healthy Fats: Olive oil is rich in monounsaturated fats, which are associated with heart health and reducing inflammation.

Flavor Enhancer: It adds depth and complexity to dishes, from a simple salad dressing to grilled fish.

Stability: Olive oil has a high smoke point, making it suitable for a wide range of cooking methods.

Versatility: Whether you're marinating, roasting, or frying seafood, olive oil is your trusty companion.

Storing Olive Oil

Keep it in a cool, dark place to preserve its freshness and flavor.

Buy in smaller quantities and use it within a few months to ensure peak quality.

Aromatic Herbs and Spices

The Mediterranean region is home to a rich tapestry of herbs and spices that add depth, complexity, and a burst of flavor to seafood dishes. Let's explore some of the stars of Mediterranean spice cabinets.

Common Mediterranean Herbs

Basil: Fragrant and versatile, basil complements a wide range of seafood, from grilled shrimp to tomato-based dishes.

Oregano: A staple in Greek cuisine, oregano adds earthy, citrusy notes to dishes like grilled fish and roasted vegetables.

Rosemary: With its robust, pine-like flavor, rosemary pairs wonderfully with hearty seafood like swordfish.

Thyme: Aromatic and slightly sweet, thyme is a great addition to seafood marinades and stews.

Spice Blends

Za'atar: A Middle Eastern blend of thyme, sumac, sesame seeds, and salt, perfect for seasoning fish and seafood.

Ras el Hanout: A North African blend of warm spices like cinnamon, cumin, and coriander, ideal for adding depth to seafood tagines.

Herbes de Provence: A fragrant mix of herbs like lavender, marjoram, and thyme, often used in Southern French seafood dishes.

With these essential ingredients in your culinary arsenal, you're well-prepared to embark on your Mediterranean seafood cooking adventure. In the upcoming chapters, we'll put this knowledge to use with a variety of delicious recipes that showcase the beauty of fresh seafood, the richness of olive oil, and the magic of Mediterranean herbs and spices.

Chapter 3: Mediterranean Seafood Cooking Techniques

In the Mediterranean, the art of cooking seafood is as diverse as the cultures that surround the sea. From the smoky allure of grilling to the succulent results of poaching, mastering various cooking techniques allows you to create a symphony of flavors and textures with your seafood dishes. In this chapter, we'll explore four essential Mediterranean seafood cooking techniques: grilling and barbecuing, baking and roasting, pan-searing and frying, and poaching and steaming. With these techniques in your repertoire, you'll have the skills to bring out the best in your seafood creations.

Grilling and Barbecuing

Grilling and barbecuing are quintessential Mediterranean cooking methods that infuse seafood with a smoky, charred flavor. Whether it's sizzling prawns on skewers or whole fish over open flames, this technique is all about capturing the essence of the sea.

Tips for Grilling and Barbecuing Seafood

Preparation: Marinate seafood in olive oil, herbs, and spices to enhance flavor and prevent sticking.

Direct vs. Indirect Heat: Use direct heat for thin fillets and smaller seafood like shrimp, and indirect heat for larger items like whole fish.

Grill Baskets: Consider using a grill basket for delicate items like fish fillets to prevent them from falling apart.

Grill Marks: For those beautiful grill marks, resist the temptation to flip seafood too early; it should release easily when ready.

Wood Chips: Soak wood chips (such as cedar or hickory) for a unique smoky flavor infusion.

Baking and Roasting

Baking and roasting seafood in the oven is a gentle and reliable method that yields succulent results. It's perfect for dishes like whole fish with aromatic herbs and flavorful baked seafood casseroles.

Tips for Baking and Roasting Seafood

Temperature Control: Preheat your oven to the desired temperature, and use a thermometer to ensure the correct internal temperature.

Use a Baking Dish: Choose an appropriate baking dish, and consider adding vegetables, herbs, or citrus slices to infuse flavor.

Parchment Paper or Foil: To keep seafood moist and prevent sticking, consider cooking it on parchment paper or aluminum foil.

Broiling: Finish by broiling for a few minutes to achieve a golden crust on top.

Pan-Searing and Frying

Pan-searing and frying seafood in olive oil or a blend of olive and vegetable oil is a classic Mediterranean technique that delivers a crispy exterior and tender interior. It's perfect for quick-cooking fillets, calamari, or prawns.

Tips for Pan-Searing and Frying Seafood

Dry Seafood: Pat seafood dry with paper towels to ensure a good sear and prevent splattering.

Hot Pan: Use a hot, well-oiled pan and avoid overcrowding to achieve a nice sear.

Flip Once: Let seafood sear on one side before flipping to the other side.

Dredging: Consider dredging seafood in flour, breadcrumbs, or a light batter for extra crunch.

Drain on Paper Towels: After frying, place seafood on paper towels to remove excess oil.

Poaching and Steaming

Poaching and steaming are gentle methods that maintain the delicate flavors and textures of seafood. These techniques are perfect for creating light and healthy Mediterranean dishes, such as seafood soups and elegant seafood platters.

Tips for Poaching and Steaming Seafood

Liquid Choices: Use a flavorful liquid like fish stock, white wine, or a combination of water and lemon juice for poaching.

Gentle Heat: Keep the poaching liquid just below a simmer to prevent overcooking.

Steamer Baskets: When steaming, use a steamer basket to keep seafood above the water level for even cooking.

Aromatics: Add aromatic herbs, garlic, and spices to the poaching liquid for extra flavor.

Timed Cooking: Pay close attention to cooking times, as seafood can quickly go from perfectly tender to overcooked.

With these versatile Mediterranean seafood cooking techniques at your fingertips, you'll be prepared to craft a wide range of dishes that capture the essence of the Mediterranean. In the following chapters, we'll put these techniques to work with a plethora of mouthwatering recipes that showcase the diversity and deliciousness of Mediterranean seafood cuisine.

Chapter 4: Classic Mediterranean Seafood Paella

Paella is a vibrant and iconic dish that hails from the coastal regions of Spain, particularly Valencia. It's a captivating medley of flavors and textures, showcasing the best of Mediterranean ingredients. In this chapter, we'll explore the essence of this classic dish, from understanding its ingredients and variations to mastering the art of creating the perfect Socarrat – the coveted crispy bottom layer.

Ingredients and Variations

Paella is a canvas for culinary creativity, allowing you to personalize it with your favorite seafood, meats, and vegetables. While there are countless paella variations, let's explore the key ingredients that make this dish quintessentially Mediterranean.

Essential Paella Ingredients

Bomba or Calasparra Rice: These short-grain rice varieties absorb flavor well without becoming mushy, creating the paella's distinct texture.

Saffron: Known as "red gold," saffron threads infuse the dish with a vibrant color and subtle floral flavor.

Olive Oil: Extra virgin olive oil is the foundation of flavor in paella.

Sofrito: This aromatic base typically includes onions, garlic, tomatoes, and bell peppers, sautéed in olive oil.

Protein: Seafood is a star ingredient, with options like shrimp, mussels, clams, and squid. Meats like chicken, rabbit, and chorizo are also common.

Seasonings: Paprika, bay leaves, and occasionally rosemary or thyme add depth to the dish.

Broth: A flavorful broth, often made from fish or shellfish, forms the cooking liquid.

Popular Paella Variations

Paella Valenciana: The original paella recipe, featuring rabbit, chicken, and snails.

Seafood Paella (Paella de Marisco): Loaded with an assortment of fresh seafood, this is a seafood lover's dream.

Mixed Paella (Paella Mixta): Combines both seafood and meats, offering a taste of everything.

Vegetarian Paella (Paella de Verduras): A plant-based delight, showcasing the bounty of Mediterranean vegetables.

Black Paella (Arroz Negro): Colored with squid ink, this paella has a unique, earthy flavor.

Paella de Fideuà: Instead of rice, this variation uses short, thin noodles.

Step-by-Step Paella Preparation

Mastering paella requires a balance of technique and patience. Here's a step-by-step guide to crafting a classic Mediterranean Seafood Paella.

1. Prepare the Ingredients

Gather and prep all ingredients: rice, seafood, vegetables, seasonings, saffron, and broth.

2. Heat the Paella Pan

Use a traditional wide, shallow paella pan (paellera) or a large skillet.

Heat olive oil over medium-high heat.

3. Sauté the Sofrito

Add finely chopped onions, garlic, and bell peppers to the hot oil.

Cook until softened and fragrant.

4. Add the Rice and Seasonings

Stir in the rice and season with paprika and saffron.

Toast the rice slightly to absorb flavors.

5. Pour in the Broth

Add the hot broth and bay leaves.

Adjust the heat to maintain a steady simmer.

6. Arrange the Seafood

Arrange seafood on top of the rice. Place shrimp and clams with their shells facing
up.

Nestle other seafood like mussels and squid into the rice.

7. Cook and Rotate

Simmer without stirring, allowing a crust to form on the bottom (Socarrat). Rotate the pan occasionally for even cooking.

8. Check for Doneness

The paella is ready when the rice is cooked and the seafood is tender. The Socarrat should be crispy and golden.

9. Rest and Serve

Remove from heat and let it rest for a few minutes.

Serve directly from the pan, garnished with fresh herbs and lemon wedges.

Perfecting the Socarrat (Crispy Bottom)

Achieving the coveted Socarrat is a hallmark of a well-made paella. It's a layer of golden, crispy rice that forms at the bottom of the pan. Here are some tips to ensure you get it just right:

Use the right rice: Bomba or Calasparra rice absorbs liquid without becoming mushy, creating the ideal texture for Socarrat.

Maintain a steady simmer: Avoid stirring the rice once it's added to the pan. This allows the rice to form a crust as it cooks.

Rotate the pan: To ensure even cooking and browning of the bottom layer, gently rotate the pan during cooking.

Monitor the heat: Adjust the heat as needed to keep the paella at a simmer without boiling or drying out.

With these techniques and tips, you're well on your way to creating a classic Mediterranean Seafood Paella that's sure to impress your guests and transport them to the sun-drenched shores of the Mediterranean.

Chapter 5: Grilled Octopus and Calamari Delights

Grilled octopus and calamari are Mediterranean treasures known for their tender texture and delicious, smoky flavor. In this chapter, we'll explore how to select, prepare, and grill these cephalopods to perfection. From buying and cleaning octopus and calamari to creating flavorful marinades and mastering grilling techniques, you'll discover the secrets to creating delightful Mediterranean dishes that are sure to impress.

Buying and Preparing Octopus and Calamari

Before you can create mouthwatering grilled octopus and calamari dishes, it's essential to choose the right seafood and prepare it properly.

Octopus Selection

Freshness: Look for fresh octopus with a firm texture and a glossy, unbroken skin.

Size: Smaller octopus (around 1-2 pounds) tend to be more tender and flavorful than larger ones.

Cleanliness: Ensure that the octopus has been properly cleaned, with the beak and ink sac removed.

Calamari Selection

Fresh or Frozen: Fresh calamari should have a clean, ocean-like smell and firm flesh. Frozen calamari can also be of high quality.

Tentacles: Calamari with attached tentacles are often preferred for presentation.

Preparing Octopus

Thawing: If using frozen octopus, thaw it in the refrigerator overnight.

Cleaning: Remove the beak, ink sac, and eyes. Rinse thoroughly to remove any sand or debris.

Tenderizing: To achieve a tender texture, you can blanch the octopus by briefly dipping it in boiling water or simmering it until tender (about 30-60 minutes, depending on size).

Preparing Calamari

Cleaning: Clean the calamari by removing the head, tentacles, and innards. Rinse well.

Tenderizing: For tender calamari, consider briefly marinating it in an acidic ingredient like lemon juice or buttermilk for 15-30 minutes.

Marinades and Seasonings

Creating flavorful marinades is the key to enhancing the natural taste of octopus and calamari and infusing them with Mediterranean flair.

Octopus Marinades

Lemon and Herb Marinade: A classic choice featuring lemon zest, garlic, olive oil, and fresh herbs like thyme and rosemary.

Spanish-Inspired Marinade: Combine smoked paprika, garlic, and olive oil for a smoky, spicy flavor.

Greek-Style Marinade: Blend olive oil, lemon juice, oregano, and garlic for a Mediterranean twist.

Calamari Marinades

Garlic and Herb Marinade: A simple blend of minced garlic, olive oil, fresh herbs, and lemon juice.

Asian-Inspired Marinade: Combine soy sauce, sesame oil, ginger, and garlic for an alternative flavor profile.

Chili-Lime Marinade: Add some heat with chili flakes and the zing of fresh lime juice.

Grilling Tips and Tricks

Grilling octopus and calamari can be a breeze with the right techniques and a hot grill.

Octopus Grilling Tips

High Heat: Octopus benefits from high heat for a quick sear. Preheat the grill to medium-high.

Basting: Brush the octopus with olive oil or marinade while grilling to prevent it from drying out.

Charred Tentacles: For crispy tentacles, grill them separately for a few minutes.

Calamari Grilling Tips

Quick Cook: Calamari cooks rapidly, so keep a close eye on it to avoid overcooking. Grill for 2-3 minutes per side.

Don't Overcrowd: Ensure there's enough space between calamari pieces to allow for even cooking.

Grill Marks: Calamari develops appealing grill marks when it's placed on a hot grill grating.

With these tips and tricks, you'll be able to create succulent and flavorful grilled octopus and calamari dishes that are sure to be the highlight of your Mediterranean seafood menu.

Chapter 6: Fresh Mediterranean Fish Fillets: A Primer

Fresh Mediterranean fish fillets are a culinary delight, known for their delicate flavor and versatility in a wide range of dishes. In this chapter, we'll delve into the world of selecting the freshest catch, explore simple and delicious fish fillet recipes, and even dip our toes into the art of cooking whole fish. Whether you're a seafood enthusiast or just starting your journey, this primer will equip you with the knowledge and techniques to prepare Mediterranean fish fillets like a pro.

Selecting the Freshest Catch

Choosing the freshest fish is the first step to creating outstanding seafood dishes. Here are some tips to ensure you select the best catch:

Characteristics of Fresh Fish

Bright and Clear Eyes: Fresh fish should have clear, bright eyes, not cloudy or sunken.

Firm Flesh: Gently press the flesh; it should spring back and not leave an indentation.

Moisture and Smell: The fish should be moist, not dry, and should have a fresh, ocean-like smell, not a strong fishy odor.

Scales and Skin: Scales should be intact and shiny, and the skin should be vibrant and not discolored.

Ask Questions

Don't hesitate to ask your fishmonger where the fish came from and when it was caught. Freshness is paramount.

Support sustainable fishing practices by choosing fish that are labeled as sustainably sourced.

Simple Fish Fillet Recipes

Fish fillets are a blank canvas for culinary creativity, and Mediterranean cuisine offers countless ways to prepare them. Here are three simple and flavorful fish fillet recipes to get you started:

Mediterranean Baked Fish Fillets

1. Preheat the oven to 375°F (190°C).
2. Place seasoned fish fillets (seasoned with salt, pepper, and herbs) in a baking dish.
3. Drizzle with olive oil and lemon juice.
4. Top with sliced tomatoes, olives, and capers.
5. Bake for 15-20 minutes or until the fish flakes easily with a fork.
6. Garnish with fresh herbs and serve.

Lemon-Garlic Grilled Fish

1. Preheat the grill to medium-high heat.
2. Marinate fish fillets in a mixture of olive oil, lemon juice, minced garlic, and fresh herbs for 15-30 minutes.
3. Grill for 3-4 minutes per side, or until the fish has grill marks and is cooked through.
4. Serve with additional lemon wedges.

Pan-Seared Fish with Mediterranean Salsa

1. Season fish fillets with salt, pepper, and your choice of Mediterranean herbs and spices.
2. Heat olive oil in a skillet over medium-high heat.
3. Sear the fillets for 3-4 minutes per side until golden and cooked through.
4. Serve with a fresh Mediterranean salsa made with diced tomatoes, red onion, olives, and herbs.

Cooking Whole Fish

While fish fillets are convenient, cooking whole fish can be a rewarding experience that allows you to savor the fish's natural flavors. Here's a basic method for cooking whole fish:

Cleaning: Ensure the fish is scaled and gutted. Rinse it thoroughly inside and out.

Seasoning: Stuff the fish cavity with herbs, citrus slices, and garlic. Season the outside with salt, pepper, and olive oil.

Grilling or Baking: Grill or bake the fish until the flesh flakes easily. Cooking times will vary depending on the size of the fish.

Serving: Whole fish is often served with a drizzle of olive oil and a squeeze of lemon or a flavorful sauce.

With this primer, you're ready to dive into the world of fresh Mediterranean fish fillets and explore their culinary potential. Whether you choose to grill, bake, or prepare whole fish, you'll find that the simplicity of Mediterranean cooking allows the natural flavors of the fish to shine through.

Chapter 7: Mediterranean Seafood Soups and Stews

Mediterranean seafood soups and stews are a comforting and hearty way to enjoy the bounty of the sea. In this chapter, we'll explore three iconic dishes: Bouillabaisse, a Mediterranean classic from Southern France; Cioppino, a flavorful Italian seafood stew; and Traditional Greek Fish Soup. These recipes showcase the rich flavors and regional nuances of Mediterranean cuisine, making them perfect additions to your culinary repertoire.

Bouillabaisse: A Mediterranean Classic

Bouillabaisse is a beloved Provençal fish stew that originates from the port city of Marseille in Southern France. It's a flavorful and aromatic dish that brings together a variety of seafood, herbs, and spices.

Ingredients:

- A mix of fresh seafood, such as red snapper, sea bass, mussels, clams, and shrimp.
- Olive oil, onions, leeks, garlic, and tomatoes for the base.
- A fragrant bouquet garni of herbs like thyme, bay leaves, and fennel fronds.
- A pinch of saffron for its signature color and flavor.
- Fish stock or broth.
- A dash of pastis or anise-flavored liqueur.
- Crusty bread or rouille (a garlic-infused mayonnaise) for serving.

Preparation:

1. Heat olive oil in a large pot and sauté onions, leeks, and garlic until softened.

2. Add tomatoes, saffron, and the bouquet garni, and cook until tomatoes break down.
3. Pour in the fish stock and bring to a simmer.
4. Add the seafood in stages, starting with the firmest varieties.
5. Cover and cook until the seafood is just cooked through.
6. Serve with a side of crusty bread or rouille.

Cioppino: Italian Seafood Stew

Cioppino is an Italian-American seafood stew that originated in San Francisco. It's a robust and tomato-based dish that showcases a medley of seafood flavors.

Ingredients:

- A combination of seafood like Dungeness crab, clams, mussels, shrimp, and white fish.
- Olive oil, onions, garlic, and bell peppers for the base.
- Crushed tomatoes, tomato sauce, and white wine.
- A blend of herbs and spices, including oregano, basil, and red pepper flakes.
- Fish stock or clam juice.
- Fresh Italian bread for dipping.

Preparation:

1. Sauté onions, garlic, and bell peppers in olive oil until softened.
2. Add crushed tomatoes, tomato sauce, white wine, and spices, and simmer until the sauce thickens.
3. Pour in fish stock or clam juice and bring to a boil.
4. Add the seafood, starting with the shellfish and ending with the white fish.
5. Simmer until the seafood is cooked through and the flavors meld.
6. Serve with fresh Italian bread for dipping.

Traditional Greek Fish Soup

Greek Fish Soup, or Psarosoupa, is a light and nourishing soup that highlights the simplicity of Mediterranean ingredients.

Ingredients:

- Fresh fish fillets, such as cod or snapper.
- Olive oil, onions, and garlic for the base.
- Potatoes, tomatoes, and carrots for added flavor and heartiness.
- A blend of Mediterranean herbs, including oregano and bay leaves.
- Lemon juice for a burst of freshness.
- Fish stock or water.
- Fresh parsley for garnish.

Preparation:

1. Sauté onions and garlic in olive oil until translucent.
2. Add diced potatoes, tomatoes, and carrots, and cook for a few minutes.
3. Pour in fish stock or water and add the herbs and spices.
4. Simmer until the vegetables are tender.
5. Add fish fillets and cook until they flake easily.
6. Finish with a squeeze of lemon juice and garnish with fresh parsley.

These Mediterranean seafood soups and stews offer a delightful way to savor the flavors of the sea. Whether you choose the rustic charm of Bouillabaisse, the robustness of Cioppino, or the simplicity of Greek Fish Soup, each dish captures the essence of Mediterranean cuisine in a warm and comforting bowl.

Chapter 8: Seafood Meze: Small Bites, Big Flavors

Mediterranean seafood meze, a delightful array of small, flavorful dishes, captures the essence of shared dining and social gatherings in the region. In this chapter, we'll explore the art of creating the perfect meze platter, along with two irresistible recipes: Grilled Shrimp Skewers with Dips and Marinated Mussels and Clams. These small bites are designed to pack a big punch of Mediterranean flavor and elevate any occasion.

Creating the Perfect Meze Platter

A meze platter is a showcase of Mediterranean culinary creativity, combining flavors, textures, and colors to create an inviting spread. Here are some key elements to consider when crafting your meze platter:

Selection of Seafood:

- Shrimp: Grilled, marinated, or served with dipping sauces.
- Mussels: Marinated or steamed in a flavorful broth.
- Clams: Steamed or served with a garlic and white wine sauce.
- Sardines: Grilled and marinated in olive oil and herbs.
- Calamari: Grilled or fried with a zesty sauce.
- Octopus: Grilled and served with a squeeze of lemon.
- Anchovies: Marinated in olive oil, garlic, and herbs.

Accompaniments:

- Dips: Tzatziki, hummus, tahini, or baba ghanoush.
- Olives: A variety of Mediterranean olives adds depth and brininess.
- Cheese: Feta, halloumi, or goat cheese.
- Bread: Pita bread, crusty baguette, or crackers.
- Fresh Vegetables: Cherry tomatoes, cucumber slices, bell peppers, and radishes.

- Nuts: Roasted almonds or pistachios for crunch.
- Herbs: Fresh basil, mint, or parsley for garnish.

Grilled Shrimp Skewers with Dips

These grilled shrimp skewers are a crowd-pleaser, and the assortment of dipping sauces adds extra excitement to the dish.

Ingredients:

- Large shrimp, peeled and deveined.
- Olive oil, lemon juice, garlic, and Mediterranean spices for marinade.
- Wooden skewers, soaked in water.
- Assorted dipping sauces: Tzatziki, harissa aioli, and roasted red pepper hummus.

Preparation:

1. Marinate the shrimp in olive oil, lemon juice, minced garlic, and your choice of Mediterranean spices (such as paprika, cumin, and oregano) for at least 30 minutes.
2. Thread the marinated shrimp onto the soaked wooden skewers.
3. Preheat the grill to medium-high heat and grill the shrimp for 2-3 minutes per side until they turn pink and slightly charred.
4. Serve the grilled shrimp skewers on a platter with a trio of dipping sauces for variety.

These seafood meze dishes are a delightful way to enjoy the flavors of the Mediterranean in bite-sized portions. Whether you're hosting a gathering or simply savoring a meal with loved ones, these small bites will create memorable moments and leave your taste buds craving more.

Chapter 9: Mediterranean Seafood Pasta Extravaganza

Mediterranean seafood pasta dishes are a celebration of two beloved culinary worlds coming together. In this chapter, we'll explore three delectable recipes: Spaghetti Alle Vongole (Clam Pasta), Seafood Linguine with Tomato Sauce, and Creamy Seafood Fettuccine. Each dish marries the rich flavors of seafood with the comforting embrace of pasta, creating a symphony of taste and texture.

Spaghetti Alle Vongole (Clam Pasta)

Spaghetti Alle Vongole, a classic Italian dish, is a testament to the simplicity and elegance of Mediterranean cuisine.

Ingredients:

- Fresh clams, such as Manila or littleneck, scrubbed and cleaned.
- Spaghetti or linguine.
- Olive oil, garlic, and red pepper flakes.
- White wine and clam juice.
- Fresh parsley for garnish.
- Lemon zest for brightness.

Preparation:

1. Cook the pasta according to package instructions until al dente. Reserve some pasta cooking water.
2. While the pasta cooks, heat olive oil in a large skillet and sauté minced garlic and red pepper flakes until fragrant.
3. Add white wine and clam juice to the skillet and bring to a simmer.
4. Add the cleaned clams, cover, and cook until they open (discard any that don't open).
5. Toss the cooked pasta with the clam sauce, using reserved pasta

cooking water to adjust consistency.

6. Finish with a drizzle of olive oil, fresh parsley, and lemon zest.

Seafood Linguine with Tomato Sauce

Seafood linguine with tomato sauce is a vibrant and hearty Mediterranean dish that showcases the flavors of the sea.

Ingredients:

- A mix of fresh seafood, such as shrimp, mussels, and squid.
- Linguine or your preferred pasta.
- Olive oil, onions, garlic, and tomatoes.
- Crushed red pepper flakes for heat.
- Fresh basil and grated Parmesan cheese for garnish.

Preparation:

1. Cook the linguine according to package instructions until al dente. Reserve some pasta cooking water.
2. While the pasta cooks, heat olive oil in a large skillet and sauté onions and garlic until softened.
3. Add crushed red pepper flakes for heat, followed by diced tomatoes.
4. Pour in white wine and fish stock, and simmer to create a flavorful sauce.
5. Add the cleaned seafood to the sauce and cook until they're just done.
6. Toss the cooked linguine with the seafood and sauce, using reserved pasta cooking water to adjust consistency.
7. Garnish with fresh basil and grated Parmesan cheese.

Creamy Seafood Fettuccine

Creamy seafood fettuccine is a luscious and indulgent pasta dish that combines the richness of cream with the ocean's bounty.

Ingredients:

- A variety of seafood, such as scallops, lobster, and crab meat.
- Fettuccine or your preferred pasta.
- Butter, shallots, and garlic.
- Heavy cream.
- Fresh herbs like tarragon and chives.
- Grated Parmesan cheese for added richness.

Preparation:

1. Cook the fettuccine according to package instructions until al dente. Reserve some pasta cooking water.
2. While the pasta cooks, heat butter in a large skillet and sauté minced shallots and garlic until softened.
3. Add white wine and heavy cream to the skillet and simmer to create a creamy sauce.
4. Add the seafood and cook until they're just tender.
5. Toss the cooked fettuccine with the seafood and creamy sauce, using reserved pasta cooking water to adjust consistency.
6. Finish with fresh herbs and grated Parmesan cheese.

These Mediterranean seafood pasta dishes offer a delightful fusion of flavors and textures. Whether you choose the simplicity of Spaghetti Alle Vongole, the robustness of Seafood Linguine with Tomato Sauce, or the indulgence of Creamy Seafood Fettuccine, each dish promises a satisfying and memorable dining experience.

Chapter 10: Oven-Baked Seafood Dishes

Oven-baked seafood dishes offer a convenient and flavorful way to enjoy Mediterranean flavors. In this chapter, we'll explore three enticing recipes: Mediterranean Baked Cod with Tomatoes and Olives, Baked Stuffed Squid, and Baked Sea Bass with Mediterranean Herbs. Each dish captures the essence of Mediterranean cuisine with a delightful blend of ingredients and flavors.

Mediterranean Baked Cod with Tomatoes and Olives

This Mediterranean Baked Cod dish is a colorful and flavorful creation that combines the mildness of cod with the bold flavors of tomatoes and olives.

Ingredients:

- Cod fillets.
- Cherry tomatoes, olives, and capers.
- Olive oil, garlic, and red pepper flakes.
- Fresh basil and parsley for garnish.
- Lemon wedges for serving.

Preparation:

1. Preheat the oven to 375°F (190°C).
2. In an ovenproof dish, arrange the cod fillets.
3. Scatter halved cherry tomatoes, olives, and capers around the cod.
4. Drizzle olive oil over the dish and sprinkle minced garlic and red pepper flakes.
5. Bake for about 15-20 minutes, or until the cod is flaky and opaque.
6. Garnish with fresh basil and parsley, and serve with lemon wedges.

Baked Stuffed Squid

Baked Stuffed Squid is a delightful dish that combines the tenderness of squid with a flavorful stuffing and Mediterranean spices.

Ingredients:

- Cleaned squid tubes.
- A stuffing mixture of breadcrumbs, garlic, herbs, and grated Parmesan cheese.
- Olive oil, lemon juice, and white wine.
- Cherry tomatoes and fresh basil.
- Toothpicks to secure the squid tubes.

Preparation:

1. Preheat the oven to 375°F (190°C).
2. Prepare the stuffing mixture by combining breadcrumbs, minced garlic, chopped herbs, and grated Parmesan cheese.
3. Stuff the cleaned squid tubes with the mixture and secure the ends with toothpicks.
4. Arrange the stuffed squid in an ovenproof dish.
5. Drizzle with olive oil, lemon juice.
6. Scatter cherry tomatoes and fresh basil around the squid.
7. Bake for about 20-25 minutes, or until the squid is tender and the stuffing is golden brown.

These oven-baked seafood dishes bring the vibrant flavors of the Mediterranean to your dining table. Whether you choose the bold Mediterranean Baked Cod with Tomatoes and Olives, the comforting Baked Stuffed Squid, or the aromatic Baked Sea Bass with Mediterranean Herbs, each dish offers a taste of the Mediterranean's culinary diversity and richness.

Chapter 11: Seafood Salads with a Mediterranean Twist

Mediterranean-inspired seafood salads offer a refreshing and vibrant way to savor the flavors of the sea. In this chapter, we'll explore three delightful recipes: Greek Salad with Grilled Shrimp, Tuna Niçoise Salad, and Seafood and Citrus Salad. Each salad features a unique combination of ingredients that bring together the best of Mediterranean cuisine and seafood.

Greek Salad with Grilled Shrimp

This Greek Salad with Grilled Shrimp is a colorful and refreshing dish that combines the classic Greek salad ingredients with the smoky flavor of grilled shrimp.

Ingredients:

- Large shrimp, peeled and deveined.
- Romaine lettuce, cucumbers, cherry tomatoes, red onions, and Kalamata olives.
- Feta cheese and fresh oregano for garnish.
- Olive oil, lemon juice, garlic, and oregano for dressing.

Preparation:

1. Thread the shrimp onto skewers and grill until they turn pink and slightly charred.
2. In a large bowl, combine chopped Romaine lettuce, sliced cucumbers, halved cherry tomatoes, thinly sliced red onions, and Kalamata olives.
3. Whisk together olive oil, lemon juice, minced garlic, and dried oregano to create the dressing.
4. Toss the salad with the dressing and top with grilled shrimp.
5. Garnish with crumbled Feta cheese and fresh oregano.

Tuna Niçoise Salad

Tuna Niçoise Salad is a classic French salad that combines tuna, vegetables, and Mediterranean ingredients for a satisfying meal.

Ingredients:

- Fresh tuna steaks, seared and sliced.
- Mixed greens, blanched green beans, boiled potatoes, cherry tomatoes, hard-boiled eggs, and Niçoise olives.
- Anchovy fillets and capers for extra flavor.
- Dijon mustard for dressing.

Preparation:

1. Arrange mixed greens on a platter and top with blanched green beans, boiled potatoes, halved cherry tomatoes, quartered hard-boiled eggs, and Niçoise olives.
2. Add seared and sliced fresh tuna steaks to the salad.
3. Garnish with anchovy fillets and capers.
4. Whisk together red wine vinegar, Dijon mustard, and olive oil for the dressing. Drizzle over the salad.

Seafood and Citrus Salad

Seafood and Citrus Salad is a zesty and refreshing dish that combines the bright flavors of citrus fruits with a medley of seafood.

Ingredients:

- A mix of seafood, such as cooked shrimp, crab meat, and scallops.
- Grapefruit and orange segments.
- Avocado slices, red onion rings, and fresh mint leaves.
- A citrus vinaigrette made with citrus juice, olive oil, honey, and Dijon mustard.

Preparation:

1. Arrange the cooked seafood on a platter.
2. Add segments of grapefruit and orange to the seafood.
3. Scatter avocado slices, red onion rings, and fresh mint leaves on top.
4. Whisk together citrus juice, olive oil, honey, and Dijon mustard to create the vinaigrette. Drizzle over the salad.

These Mediterranean-inspired seafood salads offer a delightful balance of flavors and textures. Whether you choose the freshness of Greek Salad with Grilled Shrimp, the classic appeal of Tuna Niçoise Salad, or the citrusy zing of Seafood and Citrus Salad, each dish is a celebration of Mediterranean cuisine and the bounty of the sea.

Chapter 12: Seafood Tagines: North African Influences

Seafood tagines bring the rich and aromatic flavors of North African cuisine to your table. In this chapter, we'll explore the art of tagine cooking, along with two tantalizing recipes: Moroccan Seafood Tagine and Tunisian Spiced Fish Tagine. These dishes are a flavorful journey to the vibrant and diverse culinary landscapes of North Africa.

Introduction to Tagine Cooking

Tagine cooking is a traditional North African method that involves slow-cooking dishes in a special clay pot called a "tagine." The tagine's unique shape allows steam to circulate, ensuring even cooking and tenderizing ingredients. Here are some key elements of tagine cooking:

The Tagine Pot:

The tagine pot has a distinctive conical lid that helps condense steam and return moisture to the dish, making it ideal for slow-cooking.

Tagine pots can be made of clay, ceramic, or cast iron. Clay tagines are traditional and can add a unique flavor to the dishes.

Slow-Cooking Technique:

Tagine dishes are typically slow-cooked over low heat, allowing flavors to meld and ingredients to become tender.

The slow-cooking process enhances the aromatic spices and herbs, creating a harmonious blend of flavors.

Moroccan Seafood Tagine

Moroccan Seafood Tagine is a fragrant and flavorful dish that showcases the bold spices and unique cooking method of tagine cuisine.

Ingredients:

- A mix of seafood, such as fish fillets, shrimp, and mussels.
- Onions, garlic, and a blend of Moroccan spices like cumin, coriander, and paprika.
- Preserved lemons and green olives for a distinctive Moroccan twist.
- Fresh cilantro and mint leaves for garnish.

Preparation:

1. Heat a tagine pot over low heat and sauté sliced onions and minced garlic until softened.
2. Add Moroccan spices and cook until fragrant.
3. Arrange the seafood in the tagine and top with preserved lemon slices and green olives.
4. Cover the tagine with the conical lid and cook over low heat until the seafood is done and the flavors have melded.
5. Garnish with fresh cilantro and mint leaves before serving.

Tunisian Spiced Fish Tagine

Tunisian Spiced Fish Tagine is a fiery and aromatic dish that showcases the bold flavors and spices of Tunisian cuisine.

Ingredients:

- White fish fillets, cut into chunks.
- Onions, garlic, and a blend of Tunisian spices like harissa, cumin, and caraway.
- Fresh tomatoes, bell peppers, and potatoes for a hearty base.
- Fresh parsley and cilantro for garnish.

Preparation:

1. Heat a tagine pot over low heat and sauté sliced onions and minced garlic until softened.
2. Add Tunisian spices and harissa paste, and cook until fragrant.
3. Layer the tagine with chunks of white fish, sliced tomatoes, bell peppers, and potatoes.
4. Cover the tagine with the conical lid and cook over low heat until the fish is cooked through and the flavors have melded.
5. Garnish with fresh parsley and cilantro before serving.

These seafood tagine dishes offer a taste of North African cuisine and the intriguing fusion of spices, aromas, and flavors. Whether you choose the fragrant Moroccan Seafood Tagine or the fiery Tunisian Spiced Fish Tagine, each dish is a journey to the vibrant culinary traditions of North Africa.

Chapter 13: Mediterranean Seafood Tacos and Wraps

Mediterranean seafood tacos and wraps offer a fusion of flavors and textures, making them a delightful and portable way to enjoy the bounty of the sea. In this chapter, we'll explore three creative and mouthwatering recipes: Mediterranean Fish Tacos with Tzatziki, Grilled Swordfish Wraps, and Falafel and Shrimp Pita Pockets. Each dish combines the freshness of seafood with Mediterranean ingredients, resulting in a perfect on-the-go meal.

Mediterranean Fish Tacos with Tzatziki

Mediterranean Fish Tacos with Tzatziki are a harmonious blend of flavors, combining flaky fish with a cooling and tangy tzatziki sauce.

Ingredients:

- White fish fillets, grilled or pan-seared.
- Small flour tortillas or soft taco shells.
- Tzatziki sauce made with Greek yogurt, cucumber, dill, and garlic.
- Sliced cucumbers, red onions, and cherry tomatoes.
- Fresh mint leaves for garnish.

Preparation:

1. Grill or pan-sear the white fish fillets until they're flaky and cooked through.
2. Warm the flour tortillas or soft taco shells.
3. Assemble the tacos by placing a piece of grilled fish in each tortilla.
4. Top with a generous dollop of tzatziki sauce.
5. Add sliced cucumbers, red onions, and halved cherry tomatoes.
6. Garnish with fresh mint leaves before serving.

Grilled Swordfish Wraps

Grilled Swordfish Wraps are a hearty and satisfying choice, featuring grilled swordfish with a Mediterranean-inspired marinade.

Ingredients:

- Swordfish steaks, marinated in olive oil, lemon juice, garlic, and herbs.
- Large lettuce leaves or flatbreads for wrapping.
- Sliced red cabbage, cucumbers, and roasted red peppers.
- Kalamata olives and feta cheese for added Mediterranean flair.
- Lemon wedges for serving.

Preparation:

1. Grill the marinated swordfish steaks until they're cooked through and have grill marks.
2. Lay out large lettuce leaves or flatbreads for wrapping.
3. Place a grilled swordfish steak on each leaf or flatbread.
4. Top with sliced red cabbage, cucumber slices, roasted red peppers, Kalamata olives, and crumbled feta cheese.
5. Squeeze fresh lemon juice over the fillings.
6. Wrap and serve as a handheld delight.

Falafel and Shrimp Pita Pockets

Falafel and Shrimp Pita Pockets are a fusion of Mediterranean and seafood flavors, featuring crispy falafel and succulent shrimp.

Ingredients:

- Falafel patties, either homemade or store-bought.
- Cooked shrimp, seasoned with Mediterranean spices.
- Pita pockets or flatbreads.
- Hummus and tahini sauce for a creamy base.
- Sliced cucumbers, tomatoes, and red onions.
- Fresh parsley and a squeeze of lemon for garnish.

Preparation:

1. Prepare the falafel patties and seasoned shrimp.
2. Warm the pita pockets or flatbreads.
3. Spread a layer of hummus and tahini sauce inside each pocket or on each flatbread.
4. Place falafel patties and seasoned shrimp inside.
5. Add sliced cucumbers, tomatoes, and red onions.
6. Garnish with fresh parsley and a squeeze of lemon before folding and serving.

These Mediterranean seafood tacos and wraps offer a delightful fusion of flavors and convenience. Whether you choose the harmonious Mediterranean Fish Tacos with Tzatziki, the hearty Grilled Swordfish Wraps, or the inventive Falafel and Shrimp Pita Pockets, each dish is a delicious and portable way to enjoy Mediterranean cuisine and the flavors of the sea.

Chapter 14: Seafood Risottos: Creamy and Flavorful

Seafood risottos are a celebration of creamy textures and rich flavors, making them a comfort food favorite. In this chapter, we'll explore the art of making the perfect risotto, along with two mouthwatering recipes: Lemon and Shrimp Risotto and Seafood and Saffron Risotto. Each dish showcases the creamy goodness of risotto combined with the delightful taste of Mediterranean seafood.

Making the Perfect Risotto

Risotto is an Italian rice dish known for its creamy consistency and rich flavor. Here are some key tips for making the perfect risotto:

Ingredients:

- Arborio rice: The high starch content in Arborio rice creates the creamy texture of risotto.
- Broth: Use a good-quality broth, such as chicken or vegetable, to enhance the flavor.
- Aromatics: Onions and garlic are often used as a flavorful base.
- Wine: Dry white wine adds depth and acidity to the dish.
- Cheese: Parmesan cheese is a common choice for its nutty flavor and creaminess.
- Butter: A touch of butter at the end adds richness.
- Herbs and seasonings: Fresh herbs, such as parsley or basil, can add a burst of freshness.

Cooking Technique:

1. Sauté onions and garlic in olive oil until softened.
2. Toast Arborio rice until translucent around the edges.
3. Add wine and cook until absorbed.

4. Gradually add hot broth, one ladleful at a time, stirring constantly until absorbed before adding more.
5. Continue adding broth and stirring until the rice is creamy and al dente.
6. Remove from heat and stir in grated Parmesan cheese and butter.
7. Season to taste with salt and pepper and garnish with fresh herbs.

Lemon and Shrimp Risotto

Lemon and Shrimp Risotto is a bright and zesty dish that combines the freshness of lemon with succulent shrimp.

Ingredients:

- Arborio rice.
- Shrimp, peeled and deveined.
- Lemon zest and juice for a burst of citrus flavor.
- White wine for depth.
- Chicken or vegetable broth.
- Butter for richness.
- Fresh parsley for garnish.

Preparation:

1. In a skillet, heat olive oil and sauté minced onions until softened.
2. Add Arborio rice and cook until translucent.
3. Pour in white wine and cook until absorbed.
4. Gradually add hot broth, stirring constantly until the rice is creamy and al dente.
5. Stir in lemon zest, lemon juice, and cooked shrimp.
6. Remove from heat and stir in butter until melted.
7. Season to taste with salt and pepper, and garnish with fresh parsley.

Seafood and Saffron Risotto

Seafood and Saffron Risotto is a luxurious and aromatic dish that combines the exotic flavor of saffron with a medley of seafood.

Ingredients:

- Arborio rice.
- A variety of seafood, such as shrimp, mussels, and calamari.
- Saffron threads for color and flavor.
- White wine for depth.
- Fish or seafood broth.
- Grated Parmesan cheese and butter for creaminess.
- Fresh chives for garnish.

Preparation:

1. In a skillet, heat olive oil and sauté minced onions until softened.
2. Add Arborio rice and toast until translucent.
3. Dissolve saffron threads in a small amount of warm water and add to the rice.
4. Pour in white wine and cook until absorbed.
5. Gradually add hot fish or seafood broth, stirring constantly until the rice is creamy and al dente.
6. Stir in a mix of cooked seafood.
7. Remove from heat and stir in grated Parmesan cheese and butter until creamy.
8. Season to taste with salt and pepper, and garnish with fresh chives.

These seafood risottos are a testament to the creamy and flavorful nature of this beloved Italian dish. Whether you choose the zesty Lemon and Shrimp Risotto or the luxurious Seafood and Saffron Risotto, each dish promises a comforting and memorable dining experience.

Chapter 15: Mediterranean Seafood Skewers and Kebabs

Mediterranean seafood skewers and kebabs are a delightful way to enjoy the flavors of the sea with the smoky goodness of the grill. In this chapter, we'll explore the art of preparing and marinating skewers, along with two mouthwatering recipes: Grilled Swordfish Kebabs and Shrimp and Vegetable Skewers. These dishes capture the essence of Mediterranean cuisine with a focus on the simplicity and elegance of grilled seafood.

Preparing and Marinating Skewers

Preparing and marinating skewers is a key step in creating flavorful and tender grilled seafood. Here are some essential tips:

Skewer Selection:

Choose sturdy and food-safe skewers, such as metal or wooden skewers soaked in water to prevent burning.

Marinades:

Marinades add flavor and help tenderize the seafood. Common marinade ingredients include olive oil, garlic, lemon juice, herbs, and spices.

Timing:

Marinate seafood for at least 30 minutes to allow flavors to penetrate. Be mindful not to over-marinate, as seafood can become mushy.

Assembly:

Thread seafood and vegetables onto skewers, leaving space between each piece for even cooking.

Grilling:

Preheat the grill to medium-high heat and oil the grates to prevent sticking.

Grill skewers until seafood is opaque and slightly charred, turning occasionally.

Grilled Swordfish Kebabs

Grilled Swordfish Kebabs are a hearty and flavorful dish that showcases swordfish's meaty texture and the smoky goodness of the grill.

Ingredients:

- Swordfish chunks, marinated in olive oil, lemon juice, garlic, and fresh herbs.
- Bell peppers, red onions, and cherry tomatoes for colorful contrast.
- Wooden or metal skewers for assembly.
- Lemon wedges and fresh parsley for garnish.

Preparation:

1. Marinate swordfish chunks in a mixture of olive oil, lemon juice, minced garlic, and chopped fresh herbs.
2. Thread marinated swordfish, bell peppers, red onions, and cherry tomatoes onto skewers.
3. Grill kebabs until swordfish is cooked through and has grill marks.
4. Garnish with lemon wedges and fresh parsley before serving.

Shrimp and Vegetable Skewers

Shrimp and Vegetable Skewers are a versatile and colorful option that pairs succulent shrimp with a variety of vegetables.

Ingredients:

- Large shrimp, marinated in olive oil, garlic, lemon zest, and Mediterranean spices.
- Cherry tomatoes, zucchini, and red bell peppers for a vibrant mix.
- Wooden or metal skewers for assembly.
- Fresh basil and balsamic glaze for garnish.

Preparation:

1. Marinate large shrimp in a mixture of olive oil, minced garlic, lemon zest, and Mediterranean spices.
2. Thread marinated shrimp, cherry tomatoes, zucchini slices, and red bell pepper onto skewers.
3. Grill skewers until shrimp are pink and vegetables are tender.
4. Garnish with fresh basil and a drizzle of balsamic glaze before serving.

These Mediterranean seafood skewers and kebabs offer a simple yet flavorful way to enjoy the grill and the flavors of the sea. Whether you choose the hearty Grilled Swordfish Kebabs or the colorful Shrimp and Vegetable Skewers, each dish is a celebration of Mediterranean cuisine and the joys of outdoor cooking.

Chapter 16: Seafood and Vegetable Ratatouille

Seafood and vegetable ratatouille is a delightful fusion of Mediterranean flavors, featuring the rich tastes of the sea combined with the colorful and aromatic elements of the classic French dish. In this chapter, we'll explore the classic ratatouille recipe, how to incorporate seafood into it, and serving suggestions to make your ratatouille a complete and satisfying meal.

Classic Ratatouille Recipe

Ratatouille is a beloved Provençal dish known for its medley of sautéed vegetables in a tomato-based sauce. Here's a classic recipe to get you started:

Ingredients:

- Eggplant, zucchini, bell peppers, tomatoes, and onions, all diced.
- Olive oil for sautéing.
- Garlic, minced.
- Fresh herbs like thyme, rosemary, and basil.
- Tomato sauce.
- Salt and pepper to taste.

Preparation:

1. Heat olive oil in a large skillet or pot over medium heat.
2. Sauté minced garlic until fragrant.
3. Add diced onions and cook until softened.
4. Add diced eggplant, zucchini, and bell peppers, and sauté until they begin to soften.
5. Stir in fresh herbs and tomato sauce.
6. Simmer until the vegetables are tender and the flavors meld.

7. Season to taste with salt and pepper.
8. Garnish with fresh basil before serving.

Adding Seafood to Ratatouille

To turn this classic ratatouille into a Mediterranean seafood delight, simply incorporate seafood into the dish. Here's how:

Ingredients:

- A mix of seafood, such as shrimp, mussels, and white fish fillets.
- Prepare the classic ratatouille as described above.
- Add the seafood during the final stages of cooking, ensuring it's cooked through and tender.

Preparation:

1. Prepare the classic ratatouille following the steps above.
2. When the vegetables are nearly tender, add the seafood to the pot.
3. Cook until the seafood is opaque and cooked through.
4. Adjust the seasoning as needed.

Serving Suggestions

Seafood and vegetable ratatouille can be enjoyed in various ways. Here are some serving suggestions:

Over Pasta:

Serve the seafood ratatouille over cooked pasta, such as linguine or fettuccine, for a hearty and satisfying meal.

With Crusty Bread:

Enjoy ratatouille with crusty bread or baguette slices for a rustic and delicious experience.

As a Side Dish:

Serve seafood ratatouille as a side dish alongside grilled seafood or meats for a complete meal.

Over Polenta:

Spoon ratatouille over creamy polenta for a comforting and satisfying dish.

With a Dollop of Greek Yogurt:

Add a dollop of Greek yogurt or crème fraiche to each serving for a creamy and tangy contrast.

Seafood and vegetable ratatouille is a celebration of Mediterranean and French cuisine, blending the flavors of the sea with the aromatic and colorful medley of vegetables. Whether served over pasta, with crusty bread, or as a side dish, it's a versatile and satisfying addition to your culinary repertoire.

Chapter 17: Mediterranean Seafood Sauces and Marinades

Mediterranean seafood sauces and marinades are the secret to enhancing the flavors of your dishes. In this chapter, we'll explore three versatile and delicious recipes: Lemon-Garlic Aioli, Romesco Sauce, and Traditional Pesto. Each sauce and marinade adds a burst of Mediterranean flavor to your seafood creations.

Lemon-Garlic Aioli

Lemon-Garlic Aioli is a zesty and creamy sauce that pairs beautifully with grilled and fried seafood.

Ingredients:

- Mayonnaise.
- Fresh lemon juice and zest.
- Minced garlic.
- Dijon mustard.
- Fresh parsley, chopped.
- Salt and pepper to taste.

Preparation:

1. In a bowl, combine mayonnaise, fresh lemon juice, lemon zest, minced garlic, and Dijon mustard.
2. Mix until well blended.
3. Stir in fresh parsley and season with salt and pepper.
4. Refrigerate for at least 30 minutes to allow the flavors to meld.
5. Serve as a dipping sauce for fried seafood or as a drizzle for grilled seafood.

Romesco Sauce

Romesco Sauce is a rich and nutty sauce originating from Catalonia, Spain, that pairs wonderfully with grilled seafood.

Ingredients:

- Roasted red bell peppers.
- Toasted almonds.
- Tomato paste.
- Olive oil.
- Garlic cloves.
- Red wine vinegar.
- Smoked paprika.
- Red pepper flakes.
- Salt and pepper to taste.

Preparation:

1. In a food processor, combine roasted red bell peppers, toasted almonds, tomato paste, olive oil, garlic cloves, red wine vinegar, smoked paprika, and red pepper flakes.
2. Process until smooth.
3. Season with salt and pepper to taste.
4. Use as a sauce for grilled seafood, such as shrimp or fish, or as a dip for crusty bread.

Traditional Pesto

Traditional Pesto is a classic Italian sauce that adds vibrant green color and herbal freshness to your seafood dishes.

Ingredients:

- Fresh basil leaves.
- Pine nuts, toasted.

- Grated Parmesan cheese.
- Minced garlic.
- Extra-virgin olive oil.
- Lemon juice.
- Salt and pepper to taste.

Preparation:

1. In a food processor, combine fresh basil leaves, toasted pine nuts, grated Parmesan cheese, minced garlic, and lemon juice.
2. Pulse until finely chopped.
3. With the processor running, gradually drizzle in extra-virgin olive oil until the pesto reaches your desired consistency.
4. Season with salt and pepper to taste.
5. Toss with cooked seafood, such as pasta with shrimp, or use as a drizzle for grilled fish.

These Mediterranean seafood sauces and marinades are versatile additions to your culinary repertoire. Whether you choose the zesty Lemon-Garlic Aioli, the rich and nutty Romesco Sauce, or the vibrant Traditional Pesto, each sauce and marinade brings the flavors of the Mediterranean to your seafood creations.

Chapter 18: Seafood Sides and Accompaniments

Mediterranean seafood dishes are often complemented by delicious sides and accompaniments that enhance the dining experience. In this chapter, we'll explore three delightful recipes: Mediterranean Rice Pilaf, Roasted Mediterranean Vegetables, and Feta-Stuffed Peppers. Each side dish adds depth and flavor to your seafood meals, creating a harmonious and satisfying ensemble.

Mediterranean Rice Pilaf

Mediterranean Rice Pilaf is a flavorful and aromatic side dish that pairs perfectly with a variety of seafood.

Ingredients:

- Long-grain rice.
- Chicken or vegetable broth.
- Olive oil.
- Onion, finely chopped.
- Garlic cloves, minced.
- Sliced almonds for crunch.
- Dried cranberries for a touch of sweetness.
- Fresh parsley, chopped.
- Lemon zest for a zingy finish.
- Salt and pepper to taste.

Preparation:

1. In a saucepan, heat olive oil over medium heat and sauté finely chopped onion and minced garlic until softened.
2. Add long-grain rice and cook until it's lightly toasted.
3. Pour in chicken or vegetable broth and bring to a boil.

4. Reduce heat, cover, and simmer until the rice is tender and the liquid is absorbed.
5. Fluff the rice with a fork and stir in sliced almonds, dried cranberries, fresh parsley, and lemon zest.
6. Season with salt and pepper to taste.
7. Serve as a side dish alongside grilled or baked seafood.

Roasted Mediterranean Vegetables

Roasted Mediterranean Vegetables are a colorful and savory side dish that complements seafood beautifully.

Ingredients:

- A mix of Mediterranean vegetables, such as bell peppers, zucchini, eggplant, and cherry tomatoes, cut into chunks.
- Olive oil.
- Minced garlic.
- Fresh herbs like rosemary and thyme.
- Salt and pepper to taste.

Preparation:

1. Preheat your oven to a high temperature, around 425°F (220°C).
2. In a large bowl, toss chunks of Mediterranean vegetables with olive oil, minced garlic, fresh herbs, salt, and pepper.
3. Spread the seasoned vegetables on a baking sheet in a single layer.
4. Roast in the preheated oven until the vegetables are tender and slightly caramelized, stirring occasionally.
5. Remove from the oven and serve as a flavorful side dish alongside your seafood entrée.

Feta-Stuffed Peppers

Feta-Stuffed Peppers are a delightful Mediterranean side dish that combines the creaminess of feta cheese with the sweetness of roasted peppers.

Ingredients:

- Large bell peppers, halved and deseeded.
- Feta cheese, crumbled.
- Olive oil.
- Fresh basil leaves for garnish.
- Salt and pepper to taste.

Preparation:

1. Preheat your oven to 375°F (190°C).
2. In a bowl, crumble feta cheese and mix with olive oil, salt, and pepper.
3. Stuff the halved and deseeded bell peppers with the feta mixture.
4. Place the stuffed peppers on a baking sheet and bake until the peppers are tender and the cheese is slightly browned and bubbling.
5. Garnish with fresh basil leaves before serving.
6. Serve as a delectable side dish alongside your seafood main course.

These seafood sides and accompaniments are the perfect complement to your Mediterranean seafood dishes. Whether you choose the aromatic Mediterranean Rice Pilaf, the savory Roasted Mediterranean Vegetables, or the creamy Feta-Stuffed Peppers, each side dish elevates your meal and adds depth to the dining experience.

Chapter 19: Sweet Endings: Seafood Desserts

Mediterranean-inspired seafood desserts are a delightful and unexpected way to conclude a seafood feast. In this chapter, we'll explore two unique and flavorful dessert recipes: Pistachio and Olive Oil Cake and Honey and Almond Seafood Baklava. These sweet endings bring a touch of the Mediterranean to your dessert table, showcasing the versatility of seafood in culinary creations.

Pistachio and Olive Oil Cake

Pistachio and Olive Oil Cake is a moist and nutty dessert that celebrates the flavors of the Mediterranean.

Ingredients:

- Ground pistachios for a rich, nutty base.
- Olive oil for moisture and a hint of fruity flavor.
- Eggs for structure and richness.
- Flour and baking powder for a tender crumb.
- Sugar and honey for sweetness.
- Orange zest for a burst of citrus aroma.
- Lemon juice for tanginess.
- Powdered sugar for dusting.

Preparation:

1. Preheat your oven to the specified temperature, usually around 350°F (175°C).
2. In a bowl, combine ground pistachios, olive oil, eggs, flour, baking powder, sugar, honey, orange zest, and lemon juice.
3. Mix until well combined.
4. Pour the batter into a prepared cake pan and bake until a toothpick inserted into the center comes out clean.

5. Remove from the oven and let it cool.
6. Dust the cake with powdered sugar before serving.
7. Serve as a unique and nutty dessert after your seafood meal.

Honey and Almond Seafood Baklava

Honey and Almond Seafood Baklava is a Mediterranean-inspired twist on the classic dessert, featuring layers of phyllo pastry, honey, almonds, and a surprise seafood filling.

Ingredients:

- Phyllo pastry sheets.
- Butter, melted.
- Ground almonds for nutty richness.
- Honey for sweetness and flavor.
- A mix of cooked seafood, such as shrimp and crabmeat.
- Cinnamon and nutmeg for aromatic warmth.
- Lemon zest for a zesty touch.

Preparation:

1. Preheat your oven to the specified temperature, typically around 350°F (175°C).
2. Layer phyllo pastry sheets in a baking dish, brushing each layer with melted butter.
3. In a bowl, combine ground almonds, honey, cooked seafood, cinnamon, nutmeg, and lemon zest.
4. Spread this seafood mixture over the layered phyllo pastry.
5. Continue layering phyllo sheets on top, brushing each layer with butter.
6. Score the top layers of phyllo pastry into diamonds or squares using a sharp knife.
7. Bake until the phyllo is golden brown and crisp.
8. While still hot, drizzle honey over the baklava and let it soak in.
9. Allow the baklava to cool before serving in small squares or diamonds.

These seafood desserts offer a unique and delightful conclusion to your Mediterranean seafood feast. Whether you choose the nutty Pistachio and Olive Oil Cake or the sweet and surprising Honey and Almond Seafood Baklava, each dessert is a testament to the creativity and flavors of Mediterranean cuisine.

Chapter 20: Hosting a Mediterranean Seafood Feast

Hosting a Mediterranean seafood feast is an opportunity to showcase the rich and diverse flavors of the Mediterranean region while creating a memorable dining experience. In this chapter, we'll explore how to plan your feast menu and set the Mediterranean ambiance to make your gathering truly special.

Planning Your Feast Menu

Creating a well-balanced Mediterranean seafood feast menu is the key to a successful culinary event. Here are some steps to help you plan:

1. Select a Variety of Seafood Dishes:

Choose a mix of appetizers, main courses, and sides that showcase the versatility of seafood. Consider grilled, baked, and pan-seared options.

2. Incorporate Mediterranean Flavors:

Embrace the Mediterranean palette of flavors by using olive oil, garlic, lemon, fresh herbs, and spices like oregano and paprika.

3. Balance the Menu:

Ensure your menu includes a variety of textures and tastes. For example, pair a light seafood salad with a hearty paella.

4. Include Accompaniments:

Don't forget sides like Mediterranean rice pilaf, roasted vegetables, and feta-stuffed peppers to complement your seafood dishes.

5. Offer Desserts:

End the feast on a sweet note with Mediterranean-inspired desserts like pistachio and olive oil cake or honey and almond seafood baklava.

6. Consider Dietary Preferences:

Cater to your guests' dietary preferences, such as offering vegetarian or gluten-free options.

7. Plan Ahead:

Prepare as much as possible in advance to ensure a smooth and enjoyable hosting experience.

Setting the Mediterranean Ambiance

The ambiance of your feast plays a crucial role in enhancing the dining experience. Here's how to create a Mediterranean atmosphere:

1. Decor:

- Use a Mediterranean color palette with blues, whites, and earthy tones.

- Decorate with fresh flowers, olive branches, and seashells.

- Consider using Mediterranean-style tableware, such as ceramic plates and colorful tablecloths.

2. Music:

- Play Mediterranean music or create a playlist featuring traditional songs from the region.

3. Lighting:

- Use soft, warm lighting, such as candles and string lights, to create an inviting atmosphere.

4. Outdoor Dining:

- If possible, host your feast outdoors to capture the Mediterranean feel. Set up a long table for communal dining.

5. Mediterranean Touches:

- Incorporate Mediterranean elements like a water feature, potted plants, or rustic wooden furniture.

6. Informal Seating:

- Consider low seating with cushions and rugs for a relaxed and authentic Mediterranean experience.

7. Mediterranean Hospitality:

- Embrace the warm and welcoming Mediterranean hospitality by greeting guests with a smile and offering small appetizers and drinks upon arrival.

Hosting a Mediterranean seafood feast is an opportunity to share the flavors and culture of the Mediterranean region with your guests. By carefully planning your menu and creating the right ambiance, you can create a memorable and enjoyable dining experience that celebrates the joys of Mediterranean cuisine.

As we conclude our culinary journey through the Mediterranean Seafood Cookbook, we hope you have discovered the rich tapestry of flavors, colors, and traditions that make Mediterranean cuisine so beloved worldwide. From the azure waters of the Mediterranean Sea to the sun-soaked villages along its coasts, this cookbook has brought the essence of this vibrant region to your kitchen.

Throughout the pages of this cookbook, we've explored the art of preparing and savoring seafood dishes inspired by the Mediterranean. From fresh and succulent seafood salads to hearty paellas, from zesty seafood tacos to creamy risottos, we've celebrated the versatility of seafood in the Mediterranean culinary tradition.

You've learned the importance of selecting the freshest ingredients, mastering essential cooking techniques, and crafting exquisite sauces and marinades to elevate your dishes. You've uncovered the joy of hosting a Mediterranean seafood feast, where flavors mingle and laughter fills the air.

As you embark on your culinary adventures, we encourage you to experiment, adapt, and make these recipes your own. The Mediterranean is a place of endless inspiration, and your kitchen is your canvas. Whether you're cooking for family, friends, or yourself, we hope these recipes bring joy to your table and a taste of the Mediterranean to your life.

Thank you for joining us on this gastronomic journey. May your kitchen be filled with the aroma of olive oil, the zest of lemons, the warmth of spices, and the love of sharing delicious meals with those you hold dear.

Buon appetito, bon appétit, and enjoy your Mediterranean seafood creations!